The Fabulous Life of Minnie the Sassy Chick:

The Egg-Straordinary Egg

This is dedicated to my
fabulous and sassy niece's,
Carly and Riley.

Love and Hugs always,
Aunt Cindy

Text copyright © Cindy Shirley, 2017.
Illustrations copyright © Cindy Shirley, 2017.
Edited by Cailey Shirley, 2017.

ISBN: 0-9986480-2-7
978-0-9986480-3-3

Published by
Let's Pretend Publishing LLC

The Fabulous Life of Minnie the Sassy Chick: The Egg-Straordinary Egg

Written by
Cindy L. Shirley

Illustrations by
Cleoward Sy

It all started one summer day when two sisters, Carly and Riley, found an unexpected surprise in their tree house. The girls were having a tea party when they noticed something odd on the window sill. It was a purple egg with pink fuzz!

Carly, the younger sister, pushed her glasses up onto her nose and took a good look at the egg.
"What in the world is that?" asked Carly.

Riley picked up the tiny egg and gave it a shake.
"Yep, it's a real egg," she stated.
The girls had never seen such a crazy looking egg before.
"This is really weird, Riley," said Carly.
"Let's take it inside and show Mom," said Riley. "Maybe she
will know what it is."

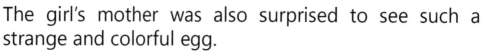

The girl's mother was also surprised to see such a strange and colorful egg.
"I have no idea what this is or what will hatch from it," she said. "Maybe you should put it back in the tree house so its mother can find it."

Not liking that idea, Riley suggested, "What if we each take turns keeping the egg in our rooms until it hatches?"
Carly was jumping up and down saying, "Please Mom, pretty please! We will do a great job taking care of this little egg. We promise!"
Finally, their mom gave in and said okay to their crazy plan. Riley looked at her sister and gave her a little wink. Carly could always get her way and Riley knew it.

Over the next few weeks, the girls continued to care for the egg. Carly came up with a special nighttime routine to follow when she was in charge. She would give the egg a warm bubble bath, blow dry its pink fuzz, and wrap it in a warm towel.

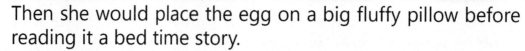

Then she would place the egg on a big fluffy pillow before reading it a bed time story.

"Now then, let's relax and get you ready for bed," Carly would whisper. "Good night, sleep tight, and don't let the bed bugs bite!"

With the egg by her side she would snuggle under a soft blanket and fall asleep.

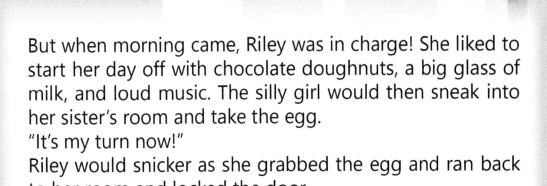

But when morning came, Riley was in charge! She liked to start her day off with chocolate doughnuts, a big glass of milk, and loud music. The silly girl would then sneak into her sister's room and take the egg.

"It's my turn now!"

Riley would snicker as she grabbed the egg and ran back to her room and locked the door.

"Time for some fun, little chickadee! Let's rock!" she would shout. Riley always snarled her lips and bobbed her head up and down to the music. After a lively round of air guitar and singing at the top of her lungs, Riley loved to gulp down an entire glass of milk. Looking into her mirror, she was always amused to see the leftover milk mustache on her upper lip.

"Well egg-cuse me Miss Egg, but you look egg-ceptionally beautiful today!" she'd giggle. "May I have this dance?"

She would then twirl wildly around her room while holding the egg in one hand and a doughnut in the other.

One day while playing beauty shop, Riley decided to brush the egg's pink fuzz and make two little pig tails. She had just taped a couple of tiny pink bows onto the fuzz when her bedroom door flew open.

"Good grief!" cried Carly. "What in the world are you doing to my precious egg?" she shouted.
Both girls laughed so loud that their mom came into the room to see what they were up to. When she saw the wild looking egg, she started laughing too!

"I have a great idea!" announced Riley.
She grabbed her camera and said, "Let's take selfies!"
"You girls are being a couple of silly woggles today,"
laughed their mom as she walked back into the kitchen.
The giggling continued as they made funny faces and
posed for crazy photos with the egg.

Once they calmed down and caught their breath, they noticed a tiny crack in the top of the egg. "Just look what you've done Riley, you broke it!" cried Carly. "No I didn't, you did!" yelled Riley. "No, you did!" screamed Carly.

Once again their mom had to come back into the room to see what was going on.
"What is the problem now?" asked their mom.

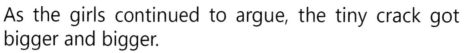

As the girls continued to argue, the tiny crack got bigger and bigger.
"Girls, look! It's hatching!" cried their mom.
They all gathered around quietly to watch.

All of a sudden out came the cutest little chick in the whole wide world. She was white with a big patch of pink feathers on the top of her head. Just above her little eyes were tiny black feathers that looked like eyelashes.

"Well just look at that!" laughed their mom. "I have never seen such a colorful little chicken before. She is adorable!"
"I know," suggested Riley. "Let's name her Minnie, the Sassy Chick!"
"That is the perfect name for her!" replied Carly.

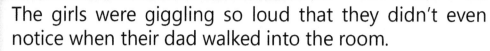

The girls were giggling so loud that they didn't even notice when their dad walked into the room.
"What in the world is going on in here?," he asked.
Their mom picked up the little chick and showed it to him.
"Meet Minnie, the Sassy Chick!," she answered. "She is our new family member."
"Well," he said, "that explains the unusual egg!"

Their dad just shook his head, smiled, and gave the girls a little wink.

"You know that you two have to take care of her every day. It is a big responsibility! You will have to feed her, bathe her, and most of all clean up after her. Do you think you both can handle it?" he asked.

"Easy peasy, finger squeezy!" shouted the girls, as they joined pinkies with their dad. "We pinkie promise!"

Their dad just folded his arms, sighed and said "Alright, I guess we can keep this sassy little chick. I can only imagine what you silly girls are going to get into together!"

Jumping up and down with excitement, the girls ran and grabbed Minnie. They gave her a big hug and said, "Did you hear that Minnie? You get to stay with us forever!"
Their adventures had only just begun!

CPSIA information can be obtained
at www.ICGtesting.com
Printed in the USA
LVOW06*1947221217
560619LV00019B/243/P

9 780998 648033